Solo
Pieces

for the
INTERMEDIATE
VIOLINIST

By Craig Duncan

Online PDF   www.melbay.com/94877EB

1 2 3 4 5 6 7 8 9 0

ALAN'S MUSIC CENTER, INC
8510 La Mesa Blvd.
La Mesa, CA 91942
(619) 466-1936

CONTENTS

On Wings of Song

Felix Mendelssohn

Espana Waltz

Emil Waldteufel

7

9

To a Wild Rose

Edward A. MacDowell

Minuet in F

Wolfgang A. Mozart

Minuet in F

Georg Friederic Handel

Bourree
from "The Royal Fireworks"

Georg Friederic Handel

14

15

Allegro

Wolfgang Amadeus Mozart

16

Traumerei

Robert Schumann

Gavotta
from Opus 2, Number 11

Antonio Vivaldi

Trumpet Tune

Henry Purcell

23

The Four Seasons - Winter

Antonio Vivaldi

Allegro
from Sonata Op. VI, No. 7

Tomaso Albinoni

Can Can

Jacques Offenbach

Air
from "The Water Music"

George Friederic Handel

Tarantella Napoletana

Italian

Marche
from The Nutcracker Suite

Peter Tschaikowsky

Solo
Pieces
for the
INTERMEDIATE
VIOLINIST

By Craig Duncan

© 1993 by Mel Bay Publications, Inc., Pacific, MO. 63069.

CONTENTS

On Wings of Song

Felix Mendelssohn

Espana Waltz

Emil Waldteufel

4

Fine

mf

p

cresc

D.C. al Fine

5

To a Wild Rose

Edward A. MacDowell

Minuet in F

Wolfgang A. Mozart

Minuet in F

Georg Friederic Handel

Bourree
from "The Royal Fireworks"

Georg Friederic Handel

Allegro

Wolfgang Amadeus Mozart

9

Traumerei

Robert Schumann

Gavotta
from Opus 2, Number 11

Antonio Vivaldi

Trumpet Tune

The Four Seasons - Winter

Antonio Vivaldi

Allegro
from Sonata Op. VI, No. 7

Tomaso Albinoni

Can Can

Jacques Offenbach

17

Air
from "The Water Music"

George Friederic Handel

Tarantella Napoletana

Italian

19

Marche
from The Nutcracker Suite

Tempo di Marcia

Peter Tschaikowsky

20